THE LITTLE BOOK OF GOOD HABITS AND BEHAVIOUR

D1642939

Written by
Alison N Roberts

Illustrated by
Michael Foley

CARROLL-DILLON PUBLISHING LIMITED

Text copyright©2006 Carroll-Dillon Publishing Ltd
Illustration copyright©2006 Carroll-Dillon Publishing Ltd

ISBN 978 - 1 - 906034 - 02 -3

Carroll-Dillon Publishing Ltd.,
28a Middle Hillgate,
Stockport.
SK1 3AY

Foreword

This book is written for junior primary school children. It is full of original poems and illustrations that help to promote awareness of social skills and social interactions.

You will also find a feelings diary, (covering one week), included to enable children to have a better understanding of their own feelings and how to communicate them to others.

We have included mazes, colouring pages and a quiz to encourage interaction and help reinforce what has been learnt.

We hope you and the children enjoy exploring the book together.

Andrew Bates, Director

Why

Is

It

Important

To

Have

Good

Manners?

TINA TANTRUM

Tina is shouting again, at her friends,
She is poking and pinching and stealing their pens.
She is pulling their hair and kicking the chairs,
And now she is stomping her feet up the stairs.

She used to be helpful and kind in her class,
She was at the top but now she is last.
When teachers are speaking she talks all the time.
Her writing is messy, it is such a crime.

She is not very grateful for being looked after,
She is moaning a lot and there's not much laughter.
She is angry that life's not going her way.
If only she'd look around, all is okay.

6

She likes to be loud to make herself heard,
But sometimes she is as quiet as a bird.
She bullies her mum and shouts at her dad,
Oh Tina, this really makes them so sad.

It started just after her brother was born,
She wasn't having much attention at home.
She began by stamping her feet on the floor,
Her granny came running right out of the door.

"Oh Tina" said Gran, "Whatever is wrong?"
She tried to calm Tina with one of her songs,
The song was a lullaby from lands far away,
Gran always sang it when things went astray.

" You have a nice home and plenty of toys,
Your friends are all lovely, the girls and boys.
And you are lucky to have food on your plate,
And a pillow to rest your head when it's late."

"Oh Granny, I don't know what I am doing,
It feels so wrong to be booing and hooing,
I know I am lucky and loved by my mother,
But I think I am jealous of my little brother."

" I am not used to sharing my mum and my dad,
And now there's a brother I'm turning quite bad.
By being mean and lonely and pushing away,
The other children that want me to play."

" Oh Tina," said Gran, "There's no harm in trying,
To act a bit better, instead of this crying,
You really are loved more than you can tell,
And helping your brother might help you as well".

"So don't be a silly girl, learn to grow up,
When you were a baby, you were as cute as a pup,
You are older and wiser than you were before,
Just promise me now that you'll try a bit more."

" Oh Gran I am sorry for this mess I've created,
I'm sorry to everyone that I have hated.
I'm sorry I've shouted and acted that way,
I'll try to be nicer and kinder each day."

THE TANTRUM MAZE

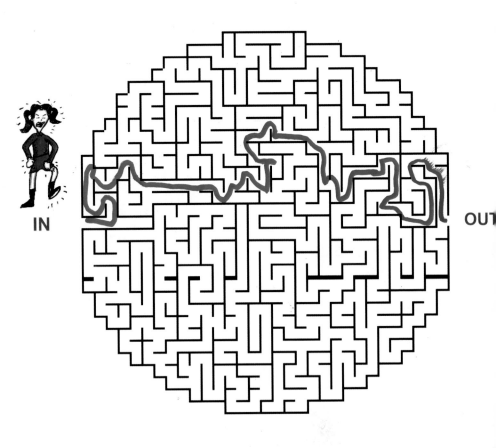

IN

OUT

Can you help Tina stop her tantrums by helping her through the maze from one side to the other?

Please and Thank You

Please and Thank you are easy to say,
When you say it to people they have a nice day.
It means you are grateful for what people do,
It means they may do it again for you.

If you say Please, when the time is right,
People will know that you are polite.
Please is a word to keep in your mind,
It helps other people to know you are kind.

When somebody does something nice for you,
What should you say? What should you do?
If you say "Thank you" for what they have done,
They will smile a big smile, as bright as the sun.

"Thank you
mum,
for doing
so
many
things
for me."

"You're welcome
darling,
It's nice
when you say
ThankYou
to me."

13

Saying Please after being asked, "What would you like?"
Saying "I would like juice Please," is very polite.
And Thank you is said when they bring it to you,
And when you are grateful for things people do.

"Please mum can I have some juice?"

"Yes darling of course you can."

"Thank you."

So practise these words, they are handy to know,
Because gratitude is really a good thing to show.
It means you have manners and you are polite,
When you say Please and Thank you, at times that are right.

PLEASE

THANK YOU

PLEASE AND THANK YOU

Can you please make your way through the maze?

IN

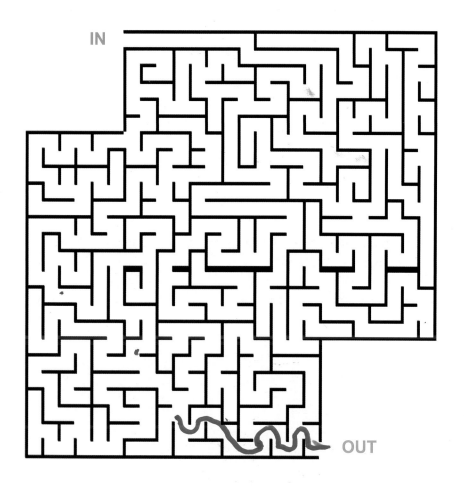

OUT

Well done, thank you.

The Story of Roger Rude

Roger is an angry boy,
He breaks the other children's toys.
He swears and shouts at home and school.
Oh, what a very naughty fool.

At school, Roger is a bully,
Never understanding fully,
What it means to be a friend,
Even now he can't pretend.

He knows inside just what he's doing,
And keeps an eye on Teacher Drewing,
Who watches out when Roger's cruel.
And pushes other kids at school.

"ROGER, Please go and tidy your room."

But Roger feels so very lonely,
No one plays because he only,
Pulls their hair or kicks their shin,
Then lets out a toothless grin.

It's all because he's not polite,
His manners are really out of sight.
He thinks it's clever to be so rude,
To stomp about in an angry mood.

But Roger needs a friend or two,
That's normal, because we all do.
He hasn't found how to be kind,
But it is sleeping deep inside.

He has an older brother who's,
Mean when Roger's not at school.
He pushes him around the room,
He even hits him with a broom.

Roger's learnt from him to punch,
And break toys with a mighty crunch.
He also learnt to push away,
The other kids who want to play.

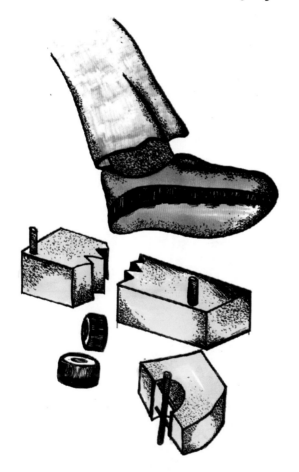

It's sad that Roger's learnt this way,
To fight, instead of nicely play.
It is a fact that if he tries,
He could learn to be so wise.

If he could choose to act with kindness,
He could overcome this blindness,
And see the friends that he could make,
By being true and not a snake.

If he can think to help someone,
He will feel nice once it is done.
A different way would stop the fight.
This happens when you are polite.

SAYING SORRY

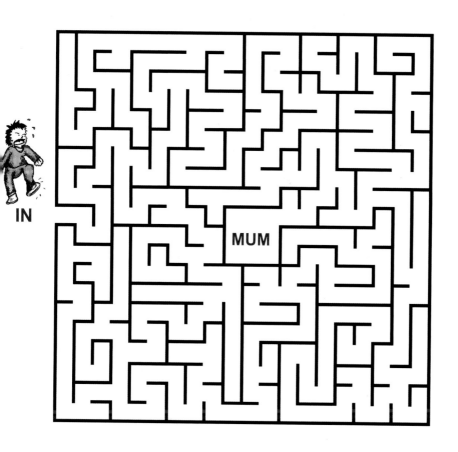

IN

MUM

Roger was very rude to his mum when she asked him
to tidy his room. He stormed off and slammed the door.
Now he is feeling bad and wants to say sorry to his
mum for being mean.

**Can you help Roger find his way to the centre of the maze
to find his mum, so he can say sorry to her?**

CAN YOU SPOT THE 4 DIFFERENCES IN ROGER'S MESSY BEDROOM?

NOW YOU CAN COLOUR ME IN

22

Saying Sorry

Saying sorry is very important if you have upset someone or been mean or rude. The main thing about saying sorry is to try NOT to repeat your mistake again.

There are many ways to say and show you are sorry, here are a few ideas.

"I'm sorry for the mean thing I did to you. I think I did it because I was feeling left out."

"I'm sorry for what I said to you, it was a very unkind thing to say. I think I said it because I was feeling angry and next time I will talk to you instead of saying horrible things."

TINA TANTRUM
SAYS SORRY

ROGER RUDE
SAYS SORRY

Saying sorry is also called apologising, it shows that you know what you did or said was not very nice and that you would like to make things better.

You know what it is like when someone upsets you or is mean. When you are unkind to someone you know how they are feeling inside because you have felt like that too.

So, if you have upset someone or been mean or rude, you could…

Say sorry and tell them why you think you did what you did and tell them that you will try not to do it again.

Or Make them a card saying sorry.

Or Say sorry to them and shake hands.

Or Say sorry and give them a hug.

Saying sorry is a good thing to do, it will help everyone feel better and it will show that you know what you did was wrong and that you are trying to make things better.

WE ALL WANT TO SAY SORRY

FALLING OUT AND MAKING UP

Making up can be hard sometimes,
but it's a good thing to **say sorry.**

MEETING AND GREETING

Meeting new people can be so much fun,
Sometimes it's scary but has to be done.
Some people are friendly, some people are shy,
Some people are curious and keep asking why?

We shake hands with people and tell them our names.
These introductions are mostly the same.
It's good to ask questions of people you meet,
At parties and playgrounds or sharing a seat.

When talking to people, we look in their eyes,
This helps to see if they wear a disguise.
We talk with our hands and make sense of words,
We hear what they're saying, like listening to birds.

If we keep practising, the easier it gets,
Try meeting and greeting on family and pets.
At first you feel silly but nobody minds,
Because, it is a skill that you'll slowly find.

HELLO

HOW ARE YOU?

NICE TO MEET YOU

GOODBYE

Talking and Listening

So we can speak and we can hear,
We have a mouth and pair of ears.
We have a tongue and voice box too,
So we can talk our problems through.

Without our ears, without our voice,
We would be given little choice.
Without them we could not explain,
What's going on inside our brain.

HAPPY

SCARED

ANGRY

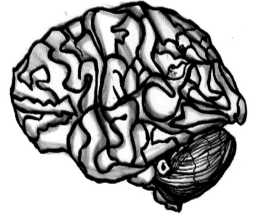

CONFUSED

SAD

**If you use your mouth to shout,
By throwing words and noise about,**

**You'll get yourself into a spin,
By making all this awful din.**

30

When you begin to realise,
That words can help to open eyes,
By telling others how you're feeling,
And choosing words that are revealing.

This is why it's good to know,
Lots of words and what they show.
To use the right words when you talk,
Is as important as when you walk.

WORRIED
and
NERVOUS

CONFUSED
and
PUZZLED

SAD
and
UNHAPPY

HAPPY
and
CONTENT

If you listen to what is said,
You may help someone out instead
Of talking like a chatter box,
As that won't help their worries stop.

"I'M SCARED OF HARD HOMEWORK"

"WHAT DO YOU THINK I SHOULD DO?"

"YOU ARE A GOOD LISTENER"

"MY DOG IS ILL"

"I FEEL SAD"

"I FEEL LONELY"

"I FEEL BULLIED"

"MY BROTHER SHOUTS AT ME"

"MY SISTER KICKED ME"

"I like trees and birds"

"I'm going to Becky's party"

"My brother has won a prize"

"I got a star for my homework"

"I love you".

With words you can pass on your views,
Express emotions, share some news.

And speaking in a caring way,
Helps others listen to what you say.

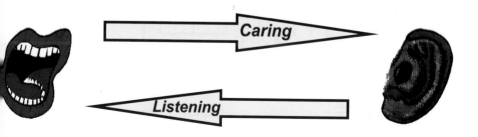

Caring

Listening

TALKING AND LISTENING

IN

OUT

Can you make your way through the
maze without **talking** but **listening**?

IF YOU...

If you see someone being mean,
Tell your teacher just what you have seen.

If you see someone trying to bully,
See your teacher and tell them fully.

If you play with matches and lighters too,
It might start a fire or really burn you.

**If you open a bottle that looks like pop,
It might be bleach so you had better stop.**

**If you find pills that look quite yummy,
Do not be tempted, they might hurt your tummy.**

If you play near water, you had better beware,
You can drown so quickly, so better take care.

If you don't look both ways before crossing the road,
You might get run over and squashed like a toad.

If you see someone strange hanging about,
Tell someone even if there is some doubt.

If you are rude and shout a lot,
You will sound like a baby, stuck in its cot.

If you are brave and use your brain,
Your fears will not drive you insane.

If you have nightmares don't forget,
It's just a dream and not a threat.

If you watch too much telly,
And eat bad food it wobbles your belly.

If you argue, what a crime,
It means you are not giving listening time.

If you read lots of books,
It gives your brain ideas to cook.

If your nightmares make you squeal,
Remember monsters are not real.

If you eat some healthy food,
You will have a better mood.

Legs and Bellies

Our bodies love to run about.
Just like our voices love to shout.
Our legs love skipping to the shop,
They love to bounce and love to hop.

But if you are watching too much Telly,
Your body gets big around the belly,
You exercise to keep it fit,
This does not happen when you just sit.

Computer and console games,
If played too much, oh what a shame.
Your body will get rounder and,
Your eyes will feel as dry like sand.

With games it means you use your eyes,
You use your hands, but not your thighs,
You sit and play some fighting scenes,
And wonder why you are feeling mean.

But exercise can be such fun,
Leaping about, playing catch and run,
Bicycles can be another way,
To help your body's health today.

And eating junk food is not good,
Your body needs fruit, as fire needs wood.
Your body needs water, sun and greens,
To be alive and full of beans.

So get outside and have some fun,
Remember how legs like to run.
Remember bodies need good food,
To stop you being in a mood.

LEGS AND BELLIES

IN

OUT

Can you help the boy with the round belly through the maze to get fit ?

Why Do We Need Lots Of Sleep, Exercise And Healthy Food?

Why do we need lots of sleep and exercise?

If you are tired and haven't had enough sleep, you may feel …

Grumpy

Have a short temper

Feel very tired

Not be able to concentrate at school

Not be very alert

Not have enough energy to play

A good night's sleep gives you. . . .

More patience

Sharper thinking

More concentration

Happier mood

More energy

If you are not getting enough exercise you may be...

More grumpy and tired

Getting bored

Feeling lazy

Putting on some weight

Lacking energy

Exercise gives you…

Sharper brain

Better health

New people to meet

Friends to play with

Your Body feels good

Your lungs can hold more air

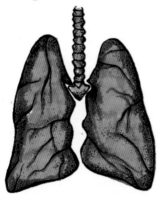

Stronger muscles

51

Why does our body like healthy food?

Just like petrol feeds a car engine so it can run, food helps
to give our body energy, so we can run, think, play
and do things without breaking down.

Some foods and drinks are better for our bodies
than others. Some food will not be so good for
your body.

The best way to eat is, eat lots of the food that is good for
you and only eat a little bit of food that is not so good
for you.

Sweets, crisps, biscuits, cakes and fizzy drinks
taste good but are not so good for you
if you eat them all the time.

Fruit, vegetables, water and juice are great
for your body. They help to keep your body
healthy. It means you won't
get so sick or too chubby and your
bones will be strong.

For a healthy life and body

Eat healthy, play a lot and sleep well.

NOW YOU CAN COLOUR ME IN

GOOD HABITS

IN

Can you find your way to the healthy food?

CAN YOU SPOT THE 4 DIFFERENCES?

YOU CAN COLOUR ME IN

56

Why

Is

It

Important

To

Let Other

People

Be

Themselves?

Everyone Is Different.

You like chocolate,
She likes peas,
He likes to scratch the back of his knees.

You like football,
She likes swimming,
She likes to have a go at knitting.

You play X-Box,
He eats jelly,

She likes flowers when they are smelly.

You like curry,
He likes rice,
She eats anything as long as it is nice.

He wears a turban,
You wear a veil,
She wears a sari, even in a gale.

You like reading,
He likes to sing,
She loves to answer the phone when it rings.

We are all humans,
Different and the same.
Let us understand with love not blame.

Why

Is It

Important

To

Let Other

People

Be

Themselves?

NEVER and ALWAYS

Never hurt a person,
Never hurt a flower,
Never hurt an animal,
It is within your power.

Always be a helper,
Always speak the truth,
Always try your hardest,
And try to brush each tooth.

Never drop your rubbish,
Never swallow gum,
Never wish for monsters,
And always wipe your bum.

Always wash your hands clean,
Always share your things,
Always try to listen,
Even when the birdies' sing.

Never shout at teachers,
Never pinch your mates,
Never go with strangers,
Outside the school yard gates.

Always eat your vegetables,
Always have some fun,
Always try to exercise,
Be careful in the sun.

Never bully others,
Never swear at all,
Never steal from anyone,
And don't draw on a wall.

NEVER AND ALWAYS

IN

OUT

Can you make your way through the maze,
never touching the sides and **always** taking care?

How

Can

You

Get

To

Know

Your

Feelings?

Freddy and his Feelings

Everybody knows that we cannot feel the same all the time and that our feelings can change.

Sometimes it is hard to find the right words to explain how we are feeling inside, but using the right words can help people understand what is happening inside us.

Some people keep a diary to write down how they are feeling. This can help us to look at what things change our moods.

Sometimes if we are tired we can feel grumpy and have a short temper, sometimes someone does something nice for us and this makes us feel happy.

Can you think of any words that help to describe the different ways we can feel?

Can you draw a line to match the feeling words to the feeling faces?

WORRIED

HAPPY

SAD

TIRED

ANGRY

Have you noticed that your body gives you certain signs when it is feeling a certain way.

By drawing a line, can you connect the body feeling with the body reaction?

Gasp	Happy
Yawn	Angry
Shout	Sad
Laugh	Tired
Cry	Shocked

Here are some words that describe how you might feel inside sometimes.

GRUMPY

HAPPY

SAD

WORRIED

TIRED

ANGRY

FEELINGS

PLAYFUL

CONFUSED

CHEEKY

UPSET

LAZY

SCARED

Can you think of any more?

FREDDY'S FEELING DIARY

DAY OF THE WEEK	MORNING FEELINGS	REASON	AFTERNOON FEELINGS	REASON
MONDAY	TIRED	Up for School	PLEASED	Good marks for homework
TUESDAY	EXCITED	Swimming today	ANGRY	Peter stole his new rubber
WEDNESDAY	SAD	His dog, Benji, has gone missing	EXCITED	He was picked for football team
THURSDAY	GRUMPY	Worried about Benji	WORRIED	His homework is very bad
FRIDAY	TIRED+ GRUMPY	Could not sleep	CHEEKY	It is nearly the weekend
SATURDAY	HAPPY	Benji has come home	PLAYFUL	Meeting up with good friends
SUNDAY	HAPPY	His dad took him bowling	LAZY	Tired after going out

Turn

Over

The

Page

For

Your

Weekly

Diary

MONDAY

THIS MORNING

I FEEL _____

BECAUSE _____

_____

_____

THIS AFTERNOON

I FEEL _____

BECAUSE _____

_____

_____

74

TUESDAY

THIS MORNING

I FEEL
_____

BECAUSE
_____

_____

_____

THIS AFTERNOON

I FEEL
_____

BECAUSE
_____

_____

_____

WEDNESDAY

THIS MORNING

I FEEL

BECAUSE

THIS AFTERNOON

I FEEL

BECAUSE

THURSDAY

THIS MORNING

I FEEL

BECAUSE

THIS AFTERNOON

I FEEL

BECAUSE

FRIDAY

THIS MORNING

I FEEL

BECAUSE

THIS AFTERNOON

I FEEL

BECAUSE

SATURDAY

THIS MORNING

I FEEL
_____

BECAUSE
_____

_____

_____

THIS AFTERNOON

I FEEL
_____

BECAUSE
_____

_____

_____

SUNDAY

THIS MORNING

I FEEL

BECAUSE

THIS AFTERNOON

I FEEL

BECAUSE

80

Paul & Sue

Answer

Some

Problems

Dear Paul and Sue,

Today at school, I saw my friend steal someone's pencil case. I am shocked and not sure what I should do next.

Please can help you me?

Thank you,

Amanda aged 6

Taking without asking is called stealing.

Dear Amanda.

It is very hard when you see a friend do something that shocks you, it feels as if you don't really know them anymore. There are a few things that you could do. You could, tell your teacher what you saw, so that she knows that your friend may be stealing and can talk to them and offer them some help.

You could talk to your friend and ask them why they did it and ask if they need help at all.

Maybe your friends' parents have no money to buy them some pens or maybe they just need to be told again that stealing is NOT a good thing to do and they could get into big trouble.

You could ask them to return the pencil case and say sorry to the person they stole from.

Or you could just forget what you saw.

But I think because you have asked for help, it means that you are worried about things and need to feel as though you can help.

Whatever you choose to do to help your friend, remember to be as kind as you can and think before you do anything.

Good Luck,
Paul and Sue

Can I borrow a pencil please?

Yes you can, thanks for asking me first

Dear Paul and Sue,

My best friend is not talking to me anymore because a new girl at school has taken her away from me.

I am feeling lonely and upset, what can I do?

Sad Suzy aged 7

Dear Suzy,

This is a very sad letter and we get a lot of letters every week from girls and boys who are going through the same thing.

It is hard to be the one who is left out but maybe this is a chance for you to meet some new friends who might be more fun and teach you new things.

Most people have had this happen to them, as well as ourselves. It doesn't mean that you are a bad person or boring, perhaps it will turn out to be a good thing and you will meet an even better best friend who will always stand by you.

Good luck,
Paul and Sue

Dear Paul and Sue,

I am being bullied by a group of boys and girls who live on our estate. I go to the same school so I am not even safe from them there.

They push me and throw my books, sometimes they call me names. I don't want to go to school anymore and I am scared to tell anyone in case I get bullied more.

Please help me Uncle Paul, I am so unhappy.

Ben aged 7

 Dear Ben,

On my desk at the moment I have 12 letters like yours. You are not alone, bullying is a big problem.

There are a few things you can do.

You can tell your teacher and parents or carers, when they know what is going, or they can start to sort things out and keep an eye on things.

The people who are bullying you need to know that it is NOT okay to bully. They need to know that they have been found out and they must NOT carry on bullying.

If they do it again, try NOT to show them that you are upset because this is what they want. So put your head up and just ignore their remarks. If they push you or spoil your things, walk away and tell your teacher or parents.

It might feel like you are telling on them but when it is about bullying this is NOT a bad thing to do. You could also keep a diary and write in it when they do something mean. This means you keep a record of what they have done and when.

Just remember that when people bully, it is a sign that they feel unhappy inside. Bullies need to make people feel bad to make themselves feel better.

I am sure you have a lot of people who love and like you, so remember that until this bullying gets sorted out. It is better to share your problems sometimes than to keep them inside you.

Remember to keep yourself safe and DO NOT try to approach the bullies if you are on your own, make sure there are people around to keep you extra safe.

Good luck,
Paul and Sue

Question Game

**Below are some questions to answer.
You can find all the answers in the book.**

1. Can you think of any ways to show you are sorry?

2. Can you think of some ways that rude people behave?

3. Can you think of some ways that polite people behave?

4. Which foods are good for your body?

5. Which foods are not good to eat a lot of?

6. How does a good night's sleep help you?

7. What does exercise do to help you?

8. How can you tell if someone is upset?

9. What can you do to help them?

10. When you meet someone new, how can you help them feel welcome?

Other publications from Carroll-Dillon

I can feel happy, I can feel safe
A safety guide for Primary Schools
Issue 1
A child protection handbook
Issue 2
A young adult protection handbook
Get streetwise safe
A guide for secondary children's issues

Sydney the Snail plays safe
An awareness book for 4-6 year old's
Reviews

" Excellent publications
Supports our Stay Safe, Anti-bullying Programme
Wonderful teaching resource."
Principal Teacher, County Dublin

" We recently received your kindly donated 39 books. The books tie in very closely with the school's anti-bullying code of practise and the healthy school ethos that we try to promote here. I look forward to receiving extra copies and being able to distribute them".
Head teacher, Primary school, Lancs

"I would firstly like to compliment you fully on your production of Issues 1. The layout, diagrams and terminology used within it are highly commendable and make it a useful publication when teaching primary classes. The fact that it also has a lot of very relevant information for parents is of great value."
Resource Teacher, Primary School, Eire

For more information on our books please contact:

Carroll-Dillon Publishing Ltd.,
28a Middle Hillgate,
Stockport.
SK1 3AY

Tel: 0161 476 2553   Fax: 0161 476 2528